THE FIRST BEING

WAFIK A. WASSEF

authorHOUSE®

AuthorHouse™
1663 Liberty Drive
Bloomington, IN 47403
www.authorhouse.com
Phone: 1-800-839-8640

Published by AuthorHouse 1/30/2012

ISBN: 978-1-4685-4386-5 (e)
ISBN: 978-1-4685-4387-2 (sc)

Library of Congress Control Number: 2012901081

To my wife and two children:

Safaa, Tony and Andrew

In the beginning was the Word, and the Word was with God, and the Word was God. The same was in the beginning with God. All things were made by Him; and without Him was not anything made that was made. In Him was life; and the life was the light of men.

John 1:1-4

TABLE OF CONTENTS

CHAPTER 1
INTRODUCTION

I t is of the utmost importance for anyone who seeks to know the origin and the source of our own existence is to have first a comprehensive understanding of the universe around us. This understanding must not only be confined to the present state of the universe but must also include the whole history of the universe. Thus in order to comprehend how we came to be in this universe at the present time, we must start first by integrating our knowledge of the universe and connect its major events and epochs in a one unified Idea (or world view). This statement is based on the fact that our present existence did not spring spontaneously out of nothing but it was the outcome of lengthy processes of development in which we acquired a great deal of physical and mental characteristics from the universe around us as well as from countless past generations of our ancestors. Our bodies and minds are the end products of a long history of physical, chemical and biological processes. Therefore in order to have a complete understanding of our present state of existence we must first comprehend the past history of thought, and of life and of the universe as a whole. The fragmentation of our knowledge has detrimental consequences on our understanding and to the conclusions we may draw from this partial and sporadic knowledge. In an age of very high level of specialization we almost lost interest in the knowledge of the master plan behind all phenomena in nature and most of us even doubt if such kind of knowledge may exist. Connecting the landmark events in the history of the universe in a one consistent Idea is the ultimate objective of this book. Closely related to this objective is to find the meaning of these events and the final cause of everything. Therefore, unlike some of those who subscribe to existentialism, I maintain that there is a meaning behind each of the landmark events which shaped the history of our own existence as well as the ultimate culmination of the history of the universe as a whole.

The three major events that I will consider in this book are the following:

1- The creation of the universe.
2- The beginning of life on earth.

3- The emergence of human consciousness and intelligence.

There are many other events that may be included in this short list. However, I will confine my investigations only to these three events and try to interconnect them into a one consistent Idea. By this approach each event may shed some light on the other two. This approach to the understanding of our universe and of ourselves may help us to resolve many problems and contradictions that beset both science and metaphysics (or religion) when studied in isolation of each other. Thus this book is about beginnings: the beginning of the Universe, the beginning of life on earth and the beginning of human thought and consciousness.

At these pivotal moments of time the new emerged out of the old, order was established out of disorder, life sprang out of dead matter and the miraculous did occur. At these momentous events we can see clearly the Hand of God at work bringing forth existence out of nonexistence and summoning beings into the realm of reality. I will try to find the force at play that brought in each stage a new phase to the realm of existence. In the final chapter I will consider the unifying force or Idea or The First Being which is the source of all beings: matter, life and mind.

The study of matter without an anticipation of the emergence of life out of some of its constituents is a futile exercise. To put it simply, it is impossible for blank matter to produce life. There must be some guiding principles that prepare matter (or some of its components) to be fit as the receptacle or the house of life. Similarly, random evolution of life forms cannot produce intelligent human beings. There must be a guiding principle along the way that points towards the appearance of the Intelligent Man. Chance is most likely to undo and plot out what it accidentally brought forth.

Finally, I will try to answer the question whether matter, life and thought are but the revelations or the expressions (to use Leibniz favourite word) of one unique Being that reveals Himself gradually and step by step. I will try to synthesise and interconnect these vastly diverse and seemingly unrelated phenomena into a one consistent plan. In this way one may finally find out the final cause of existence. To summarize the final conclusion of this book one may say that the First Being Abode is an archetype cosmos made up of an infinite number of beings of simple substances. These beings may be identified with Leibnitz Monads. Each of these Monads is an image and a power of the First Being. The First Being is infinite in His power. Thus these entities are the manifestations and expressions of the attributes of God, the Infinite One. A cataclysmic event did occur which led to the annihilation of one of these Monads. This event is beyond the horizon of our memory and of our understanding. Therefore this event cannot be expressed by any of our languages (including mathematics) or explained by means of any of our scientific theories. We may vaguely comprehend it only in religious terms and specifically within the Christian belief. What we call the creation of the universe is nothing else but the death or the annihilation of this Monad. A monad, since it was created, could also be annihilated as Leibnitz said. Creation and Annihilation, Life and Death are but the two faces of one and the same reality. Our universe is the remains and the lingering memory of this Monad. In the fullness of time this primeval being started to rise up again and was resurrected from the ashes of the universe: First in the form of living creatures and ultimately He made Himself to be known in the consciousness of man. As if in an attempt to gather together His dispersed and broken body and to recall and recollect His faded memory He created human consciousness and intelligence. Thus the ultimate objective of our knowledge is to recall and to remember the First Being the Origin of all beings. This is the plan by which the First Being is resurrected and comes back alive again. In the fullness of time He revealed Himself by taking a Material body full of Life and Wisdom.

This theory or Idea means that species do not evolve randomly and by chance. Instead of what we call Evolution we must start to be acquainted with the idea of the gradual Revelation of the First Being throughout the history of the universe. Consider a tree for example. It starts to grow from a small seed then puts roots and green shoots, then a stem and branches, then it grows leafs and flowers. Finally it produces its fruits. We do not think of this process of growth as an evolutionary process but rather as a definite and precise process that leads to a final product that has a purpose. In a similar way we would like to connect the consecutive phases of the universe in order to anticipate its culminating end. This interpretation may explain what man is trying to do for millennia, sometimes through religious ceremonies and in other times in myth and in modern times in the study of metaphysics and by scientific theories in cosmology. Man is trying to remember certain primordial events that happened long time ago but he cannot grasp their meaning. These events shaped everything in the universe including our bodies, minds and consciousness.

This book is an attempt to synthesis our modern knowledge in physics, cosmology, biology and philosophy into a one consistent story and to combine this knowledge with other human endeavours such as religion. It is the story of our own existence. Through this interpretation we may be able to answer the following questions:

- What is the nature and attributes of the First Being?
- How was the universe created?

- What is the purpose and meaning of life (and of death)?

- What is true knowledge and what is its objective?

But where to start the search for this First Being and in what realm did He choose His eternal abode?

We notice that life requires specific structures of matter, whether we call it DNA or any other related molecular structures. Among the almost infinite possible combinations of organic and inorganic chemical compounds only one or few of such molecules are the bases of life. All forms of life share these specific structures. Again among all forms of living creatures only one creature possesses thought in its full sense. This is the human being in his full maturity. Therefore the rule of progress is clear. If we use the language of set theory in mathematics we may say that: among the universal set of all material compounds only one subset gave rise to Life, and among this subset of living creatures only one member possessed thought. Therefore the next and final step is clear and obvious: among all the thoughts and ideas that ever crossed the minds of all thinkers throughout history there is this one Thought or Idea which is the Master Idea. It is the thought behind all thoughts and the wisdom searched for by all wise men. This Idea must be called God and this First Being must be God. God chose our minds as His abode and dwelling place.

The belief in gods literally moved mountains when people erected temples and pyramids as expressions of their faith. The belief in gods gave extended life to civilizations, such as the case of the ancient Egyptian civilization, which spanned few thousand years. For the sake of God millions of believers gave their lives willingly to preserve their faith similar to what have happened to the early Christians. Can there be any doubt about the overwhelming power of this single Idea? As a matter of fact, we cannot even call it an idea any longer as much as we cannot call life by the name of the molecules of matter which support it, or call thought as living due to the thoughtful living human beings. It must grow out from its base or host, that is the mind, and a new phase must emerge out of thought. Matter gave birth to Life, and Life produced thoughtful human beings. Now thought when it reaches its pinnacle must give birth to something beyond thought but must also be rooted in thought. Those who believe in God and dismiss the mind as the seat of their belief have missed the whole nature of God. Can we find any living creature without a material body? Similarly we cannot believe in God without thought. Our mind is the house of God as much as certain biochemical molecules are the houses of Life. But God is not an Idea.

The First Being must have been there at the moment of the creation of the material universe before any human mind existed. It must have witnessed as well the gathering together of the atoms and molecules to form the first living organisms. And in His final Epiphany He made His presence felt in the minds of the first thinkers. No other idea has ever survived from time immemorial before any civilization has appeared except this one single notion we call God. We can still see those primitive people in their burial pits in the sand with little representations of their gods buried with them in the hope of the resurrection from the dead. This is a very significant fact. When we search for God we must look for Him at the earliest times because if He exists, as I and many others believe, He must have been there at the dawn of Time, at the first moment of creation and in the beliefs of the earliest people. The First Being was the origin of all beings.

When I say: I exist, what do I mean by this I? Is it my material body or my living soul or my thinking mind or perhaps all of them together? Is this I confined in this region of space occupied by my body and at this particular moment when I utter these words?

To answer these questions we have to reflect on the whole spectrum of existence. Let me first give an illustrating example: When I board an airplane and this airplane takes off and flies high in the sky. At this moment I may say that I am flying. Of course what I mean is that the airplane is flying and since I am inside this airplane then I may consider myself to be flying as well. Now let us reflect on the statement: I exist. The language I am using in this statement was developed by many generations long time ago and was taught to me by many people. Again I have to be a living and intelligent person to communicate this statement with other living and intelligent people. However, my life and my genes were inherited from my parents and from countless past generations and this material body was borrowed matter from the universe itself and so on. Therefore I find my existence entangled in a web of other existents connected and overlapping until it would be very difficult to distinguish my own existence from all of the others. Does this mean that this I has now been dissolved into an infinite series of other living and non-living entities and is extended to the farthest past that I can hardly recall? And if every other I is treated in the same way then what distinguishes me from you?

There must be a balance between the differentiation between this I and the rest of other existents and at the same time I must also integrate and extend this I to include other existents which are the efficient causes of creating and developing it. I owe my existence to many other existents but in particular to the First Existent.

To severe ourselves from the rest of the universe is the first step in the long process of our death. Life, by definition, is an integrating processes and coalescence of many elements and components, hence the complexity of all living beings. Even the most primitive living organisms exhibit such phenomenal complexity. Not only primitive forms of life require extended structures of myriads of molecules, but higher forms of life depend on a chain of many living and non-living objects. These examples of interdependence of all things for their existence and survival indicate that our own existence cannot be discussed in a vacuum or cannot be understood without reference to other existents.

Therefore when I speak about my own existence I must add to it several other orders of life and thought which made it possible for me to utter the words: I exist. Thus to make this statement more precise and complete I must add: I, by the power of the Creator, do exist. I, by the love of my parents, became alive. I, by the mind given to me by the Omniscient, ponder on this problem. Although I need to add to myself other parts of the universe, yet I cannot add to myself the whole universe at once. This finitude is the origin of the differentiation between me and you. I am this part of the universe (space and matter) and you are another part, I think these thoughts and you have your own mind. But more important, this finitude is the origin of the differentiation between this I and God. God must encompass the totality of all Existence and Reality. I am only this single existent. He must be the perfection and completeness of thought and knowledge. I only know partially. God must be Life itself in its fullness. I must have a finite life. Life itself cannot die, and complete thought cannot err or search for knowledge. God is not only the totality of things but He is also the totality of Time. He was and is and is to come, the Almighty as St. John wrote in the Book of Revelation.

No wonder, then that in the search for God I found myself compelled to discuss a vast array of subjects extending from matter to life to thought. The confinement of our knowledge to a narrow area of thought expels God out of our minds. For example we cannot find any notion of God in the study of molecular bonds between atoms or any other mundane subject. It is only in the totality of knowledge that we find some glimpse of God. God is the Universal of all universals. All particulars which are not developed in order to point to a universal lead to the denial of the existence of God. For this reason our age of materialism and narrow specialization lost the belief in any god.

Chapter 2
Metaphysics

After completing his treatise on physics, Aristotle thought to proceed and investigate the primary causes or first principles of all things that exist. Thus he wrote what came to be known as his treatise on metaphysics. In that work Aristotle devoted his investigations for the study of being qua being not in any special or qualified sense. Since then the names metaphysics and metaphysical arguments assumed a completely different and perhaps opposite meaning to what was originally intended for such an advanced science. These names, unfortunately, came to have negative and sometimes derogatory connotations. Nowadays, metaphysics is not only sharply separated from physics, the subject it intended to complete, but also is used to imply unscientific thinking.

Although many philosophers came to its rescue,

nevertheless the general impression for the majority of scientists remained the same. One reason for such attitude is that metaphysics did not achieve much progress in the last few centuries similar to what physics did achieve. But this reason is not sufficient to disdain from the study of metaphysics. All great endeavours are painstakingly slow in their progress. When one aims to climb a higher summit he must be willing to proceed more slowly and be prepared for more hardship along the way. In the light of recent discoveries in cosmology concerning the beginning of the universe, metaphysics must assume a more important role than before. One of the objectives of this book is to try to restore the original goals of metaphysics from the same point of view of Aristotle and to re-establish its natural and necessary links with physics. Aristotle called metaphysics the first philosophy. It must indeed precede physics in order to establish the fundamental principles upon which all physical laws are established, such as the notions of matter, space, time, change and causality. Among many landmark works on metaphysics, beside the work of Aristotle, the works of Leibniz, Kant and Heidegger will be referred to frequently.

The fundamental questions of physics lie beyond the scope of physics and yet must be rooted in physical phenomena. The great progress in physics in the twentieth century must rekindle a renewed interest in this important branch of philosophy. The progress in metaphysics may shed some light on some of the most puzzling questions in physics and cosmology.

The fundamental question of metaphysics is: What are the grounds and attributes of being qua being. The most common and universal attributes among all existing things, as Aristotle stated, are being and one. Every existing thing "is" and is "one". Aristotle was looking for the most universal attribute of all existing things. He tried to find out their "substance" or "essence" or the primary causes of their existence. Physics offers one answer among at least four which were proposed long time ago, namely, materialisms. The substance of all existing things, a physicist might answer and say, is their atomic and sub-atomic structures. In this case substance became synonymous with substratum or material cause. In generalizing this view, one might add also energy and its quanta. But this view will run into some difficulties once we reflect on the moment of the creation of the universe. Did matter (and energy) exist from eternity or were created at this moment? If we answer, from eternity we must explain why the universe was created at a certain moment of time after the elapse of an eternity? Why this event occurred at this particular moment not before or after? On the other hand if we answer: it was created at a certain moment of time, we have to answer the perennial question: Out of what? Out of nothing, out of the void, or a false vacuum as the physicists claim? As if by giving a name to the thing that preceded the creation of the universe, the problem is to be considered solved. Because we may ask the same question: if this vacuum existed from eternity why it did not remain as it was before the universe was created? Why this vacuum produced the universe at this moment?

So let us call the "thing" which preceded the creation of the universe and was the cause or source of its creation The First Being and then investigate the nature and attributes of this entity. It may turn out to be nothing or non-being or vacuum. On the other hand it may turn out to be the most real of all beings. As a matter of fact it must be the source of all things that exist. Non-being cannot produce being. Everything must produce out of its own nature. Being is prior to not-Being as Aristotle stated.

Thus we may state the most fundamental question in metaphysics as follows:

What is the nature and attributes of the First Being who summons all things to the realm of existence and grants them endurance, and when He abandons them they fall back into non-being?

But this question implies that things do not come into existence by themselves. Is it necessary for an entity to be the cause of the existence and non-existence of all things? Is it necessary for an entity which is not a thing among other things to pre-exist before the universe? If the answer to this question is in the affirmative, then this entity must be beyond existence and non-existence. The act of this entity must be the act of creation of existents and duration.

What is the relationship between this First Being and the emergence of life and mind? Does this Being reveal Himself in stages: now in the material universe, then in life forms, and ultimately in the consciousness and the mind of man? All these questions must be addressed if we are to answer completely the fundamental question of metaphysics as stated above.

We observe that for the study of the phenomenon of motion and change of state (acceleration), Isaac Newton found it necessary to use the concept of Force. Things do not change their dynamical states just by themselves without being acted upon by an external agent represented by an external force. If such little changes of states require something else outside the system under consideration, are we going to assume that these systems came into being just by themselves? And even far more drastically are we going to assume that the whole universe came into being just by itself or out of nothing? There must be an entity outside the realm of existence and non-existence that bestows and withdraws existence from things and consequently they come into being and out of being. But if this entity, necessarily is beyond existence then it must not be a created thing otherwise we have to look for another entity prior to this entity *ad infinitum*. But how can anyone comprehend an entity which is beyond existence? All our experience is gained from existing things. Perhaps an illustrating example may help us to understand this idea. Imagine a horizontal line drawn on a sheet of paper (as an x-axis for example). Let the area above this line represents positive quantities (positive y co-ordinates) and that below this line represents negative quantities (negative y co-ordinates). This line then separates the positive values of the y co-ordinates from the negative values. Let the positive area represents existence and the negative area represents non-existence. Therefore this line (the x axis itself) is neither positive nor negative. It neither represents existence nor non-existence. This entity (which is represented by the x-axis) separates being from non-being according to our metaphor. Moreover, as this horizontal line moves upward it changes certain area which was above this line and positive to become under it and negative (in their y co-ordinates) and according to our metaphor, it changes things from being into non-being. The opposite process occurs as well when the line moves downward which represents things coming into existence. The line represents the entity that neither comes into existence nor out of existence. It is the measure of existence. In a similar manner we are seeking to know the entity which is the measure of existence. This entity neither comes into existence nor falls out of existence. It is beyond existence.

The nature of a thing is revealed by its activities. The act of the First Being is to bring things into being. In bringing things into existence it bestows on them endurance as well. It preserves them.

Why does this entity bestow existence on certain things but not on others or none at all? Why does it offer them contingent existence or endurance for a limited duration of time and not for all eternity?

The first step in our attempt to answer these questions is to identify two distinct and independent states namely those of being and those of non-being. We may illustrate the independence of these two states by a more accurate representation than the metaphor given above, namely by two perpendicular or orthogonal axes forming an abstract plane: one axis represents being and the other perpendicular to it and represents non-being. Any point in this abstract plane has a certain component of being and another component of non-being, similar to the Cartesian co-ordinates in plane geometry. The rotation around a third axis perpendicular to this plane changes the values of these co-ordinates, i.e. from being to non-being and vice versa according to our new metaphor. Things increase or decrease in the intensity of their being. Therefore if all the realm of being and non-being is represented by this abstract plane, what name and meaning should we give to this abstract third axis? It is a dimension beyond the plane of existence and non-existence. The act of creation and annihilation is represented here by a rotation around this mysterious third axis. Change in its most general form is a transition from being into non-being or vice versa. For example a body at a certain place changes by not being at this place when moving to another place; or a body being white changes by not being white when changing its colour and so on.

What name should we give to this "third axis" or dimension which is beyond the plane of being and non-being? We cannot visualize the higher level of reality which this axis represents. Historically time was determined by the apparent rotations of the sun and stars across the sky. Could it be that there is a Universal Time that measures the transitions from being to non-being and vice versa through the rotation in the plane-of-existence around this third axis? In this case the act of the creation of the universe assumes a special meaning and becomes a reference point on this Universal Time scale. Before the creation of the universe we cannot speak of existence or even of non-existence or space, time, energy or matter. At the moment of creation we are at the point of origin of this abstract three-dimensional space. From here things spread out, from this point of origin and across this plane-of-existence, like ripples on the surface of a pond. They come into existence and out of existence. They increase or decrease in the intensity of their existence.

Consider these illustrating examples: the rotation of

the earth around its axis produces day and night, and the rotation of the earth around the sun produces the seasons. Similarly there must be an archetypal time or a Universal Time that produces an abstract movement represented by the transition between being and non-being.

This abstract movement is not an ordinary movement at all. We use the same word for the lack of a special word for it. It must be conceived to take place prior to the creation of space, time, energy and matter. In the absence of such notions no movement could have ever taken place. Therefore the creation of our universe must have been an abstract movement of a very special kind indeed. It was the prototype act of change which predated all other acts of change. But how were things brought forth into the realm of being? What magic or power is required to accomplish this act? Why things did not remain forever in the realm of non-being and nothing could have ever existed at all as Leibnitz and Heidegger had wondered? After all, as the physicists know, all things tend to stay at the state of lowest energy or ground state and non-being or the void is a state of absolute zero energy (not even the quantum ground state or the vacuum state and its quantum fluctuations). This leap into the realm of being requires external intervention. The law of conservation of energy for a closed system forbids things to jump into states of higher energy without an external source that supplies this extra energy. For example a hydrogen atom cannot make a transition from its ground state (lowest energy) into any of the higher energies of the excited states unless it absorbs a photon or collides with other particles. If this simple phenomenon requires the intervention of an external system to make this trivial transition are we going to believe that the whole universe came into being out of nothing and without the intervention of any external agent?

Quantum mechanics seems to teach otherwise and contrary to these ideas. We learn about quantum fluctuations, the uncertainty principle as applied to time and energy and the creation and annihilation out of and back to the vacuum state. Quantum mechanics answers our question about the creation of the universe by stating that, according to the uncertainty principle, if we shrink time to a sufficiently short interval one may borrow sufficient energy, out of the vacuum state, even to the extent of the total energy of the whole universe. Thus the universe may be created in this way out of nothing. As if by shortening this interval of time the violation of the law of conservation of energy seems to be less violated or more acceptable. This is similar to the argument that if a thief stole (or according to this point of view, borrowed) something very quickly and returned it back this may diminish his (or her) crime and the fact that he broke the law.

The First Being

In order for the first entity not to be a thing among all other things in the universe it must be completely devoid of any form of energy. Every existing system must possess energy in some form or another. Therefore the source of all existing systems must be different from them all, that is to say it must have absolute zero energy (or mass). Plotinus called this source the One. The One, he said "is all things and no one of them; the source of all things is not all things..... It is precisely because that is nothing within the One that all things are from it : in order that Being be brought about, the source must be no Being but Being's generator, in what is to be thought of as the primal act of generation".

But doesn't this imply that the universe came out of nothing, out of the void?

Not necessarily. Let us define another property and represent it by the symbol Y which is the inverse of energy (I call it the Ygrene, energy spelled backward). Thus the less energy a system possesses, the more value of Y it assumes and vice versa. At the limit when the energy (in all its forms) is exactly zero, then this system must have an infinite amount of the property Y. Therefore we must investigate first this property Y for any system and especially whether this Y is related to the existence of all things. In this case the First Being (which is devoid of all energy, and consequently has infinite value of Y) must be the most real entity. Moreover if we prove that no other system beside the

Primordial entity may assume infinite value of Y, then we may at last answer the question: Why all things in the universe must have some energy and consequently must be in a state of motion and flux? One may answer this question and say that the energy E of any system is finite because

$E = 1 / Y$

and since Y is not infinite for any being except the First Being.

Aristotle argued from the necessity of a cause of movement and he arrived at the concept of unmoved prime-mover. Similarly I argue for the cause of all the energy in the universe and arrive at the cause which is devoid of all forms of energy.

Leibniz also enquired why there are beings rather than nothing? In our present investigation we ask: What are the attributes of the First Being, the source of all beings. Heidegger asked about the grounds of being. Therefore if there is a first entity that produced all existing things in the universe we may reformulate Heidegger's question as follows: Why this first entity decided or willed things to be rather than nothing at all to exist. We ask about the will and purpose and the Master Plan that necessitates the existence of beings rather than nothing at all to exist.

We may speak about the existence or being of things but when we talk about this First Entity, we must transcend the idea of being or existence. We have to address the question of the nature or will of this entity.

If we say that the will of this entity is to grant existence and endurance to all things, we still have to understand why?

If we say that the nature of this entity is to create things, we have to answer why at this moment of creation not before, not from all eternity, not ever?

If at a certain moment then its nature was different before this moment when it did not create anything. Then its nature is changing and this requires time. And if we say that it created things from eternity we make those created things co-eternal with this entity, and this entity would not be prior and the cause of all things.

For what purpose did this entity bring beings into existence? To toy with them for a while then destroy them like a child with his toys? May be for a higher purpose? Perhaps even for a personal reason (related to the Creator Himself)?

Some metaphors were introduced long time ago to answer this question.

Is the universe playground in which events have an arbitrary meaning? Or is it a gambling table on which things happen according to sheer chance? Or is it a dancing floor upon which everything is in flux and in an eternal dance? Many people subscribed to each of the above metaphors and many others. Plato proposed another metaphor. He considered the universe as a temple in which its Creator has His resting place. In this case the creation of the universe at once has a meaning and a purpose. The Creator of all things did not contemplate any other or external things to create or to destroy. The creation of the universe was an act very much intimate to the Creator Himself. This universe is nothing else but the remains of the Body of its Creator. However, when the Body of the Creator started to be resurrected, Life emerged from dead matter and Intelligence flourished among primitive people.

We may understand the meaning of the creation of the universe by the study of the greatest of the creating minds of all ages and advanced civilizations and their achievements. Since time immemorial people devoted all their resources and strained all their knowledge and energies in order to erect temples to their gods. Could it be that these acts of creation are miniature images of the primal act of the creation of the universe itself? Could it be that man in his creations is trying to mimic God? But if the universe is a temple then to which God was this temple erected? What is the nature and attributes of this God?

Not only the building of a temple is an act which resembles the creation of the universe, but also the destruction of a temple came to symbolize the end of the world. Notice when the disciples showed Jesus the buildings of the temple in Jerusalem and He said to them: "There shall not be left here one stone upon another that shall not be thrown down". When the disciples heard these words they immediately asked him about the sign of his coming and "the end of the world". This is a very significant correlation. We may only understand the purpose of the creation of the universe when we understand the highest and noblest of our own creations such as the building of temples and cathedrals.

The universe is a temple and its galaxies and clusters of galaxies are its pillars. Its corridors are the lanes of Memory and Time.

Where then, is its holy of holies?

Where are its sacred inscriptions? Who is able to decipher and read them?

The meaning of things, why things are the way they are but not otherwise? What is the Master Plan and what is the purpose of the creation of the universe? If we know the purpose of things around us we would try to align our acts to fit into the scheme of all things and to find our place in such a plan. Imagine, for example, if a student attending a school assumes that his school is just a playground. How does this understanding affect his attitude towards his school? Or assume that this student came to the conclusion that his school is a place for mental torture. What a devastating effect could this understanding has on his whole career?

We must know why we are here? Who planned the

events throughout the history of the universe? Perhaps if we do not find the answers to these questions or ignored this plan or opposed it this might be detrimental to our very own existence. On the other hand if we try to live in harmony with the purpose of our existence a new dawn of unprecedented civilization would be awaiting for us.

To know the nature and attributes of the First Being that caused all things to come into existence is the sure thing to know why things are the way they are and to know the Master Plan.

Where is the abode of this First Being? Which way leads towards Him? Is it out there or within us in our thoughts and consciousness or everywhere?

In the beginning God created heavens and earth. For those who say that the universe came out of nothing, do they call God nothing? God forbid.

In the beginning was the Word. Those who ignore the noun in this verse, "the Word", and keep silent about this First Being, do they equate The Word with the void? God forbid.

The entity we are seeking must have been there in the beginning. This is His first attribute. Before the universe was, He was there. Before anything was created, He was there. But the verb "was" requires time. Kant used the term *"a priori"* to such attributes that are necessary and universal. Since this entity is prior to all existents therefore He must be the most necessary and the most universal of all entities. He is indeed the Universal of all universals.

Thus to answer the Fundamental Question in Metaphysics about the attributes of the First Being we may say that He has three fundamental attributes:

1. He must be incorporeal or immaterial since He is devoid of all forms of energy (or mass).
2. He is changeless or immutable since energy is the source of all forms of change.
3. He must be infinite, since His main attribute is the inverse of energy.

But how to relate this attribute we called Ygrene $Y = 1 / E$ to time and how this Entity is the source of the universe?

Chapter 3
Time

What (or who) is the primary cause for the existence of all things? Suppose that A is the cause and B is the effect. Then A must precede B. Thus Time must exist. Suppose that A's act is the creation of B. However, for every action there must be a reaction equal in magnitude and opposite in direction or sense. The opposite of the act of creation is annihilation. Does this imply that the creation of B by A necessitate the annihilation of A after its act of creation? In other words B may be just the transformation of A: A disappeared in order that B may appear in its place. If this is so, then how may we be able to reconstruct A from the knowledge of B? We may achieve this through the study of the history of B and its evolution, in particular its early history after the act of its creation since the memory of its progenitor may still persist and could be recovered from there. But Memory implies Time.

The study of the history of the early universe holds the key for the reconstruction of its source. The early universe was much smaller in size, much hotter, contained simpler elements and was in almost complete thermal equilibrium (almost uniform temperature). From this information we may conclude that if there was any source of the universe it must have been without spatial extension, that is to say it must be prior to the creation of space, it must also have been the simplest entity that is to say it must have been the absolute One that had no parts or divisions. Multiplicity requires spatial extension and the pre-existence of unity. The One must be prior to the Many. Again it must have been in a super equilibrium state, a state of absolute rest. After the moment of creation the universe acquired spatial extension and multiplicity and tremendous explosive energy that started and maintained its expansion and change. However the universe preserved some of the attributes of its source through the memory of its initial state. To preserve the memory of its prior, Time has always to be there.

The moment of creation was also a moment of annihilation. The violent explosion of the universe at the moment of its creation speaks of a cataclysmic event which probably had led to the annihilation of the source which created it. If this is so, then how to get any glimpse of the progenitor of the universe? How to acquire any knowledge about the attributes of this First Being which brought the universe into existence?

We may start our search by positing some postulates:

1. An entity prior to the universe did exist.
2. This entity was the cause of the creation of the universe.
3. This entity was annihilated at the moment of the creation of the universe.

The third postulate speaks of "the death of the Creator, by whom all things were made", a theme repeated again and again in Christianity and in other religions as well.

The First Being did not leave behind disciples or written records or erected monuments. How then can we learn anything about this entity if it did ever exist?

If He did create the universe then the universe must bear witness to Him. It must preserve and keep some memory of Him. Let us then search for such memory everywhere from elementary particles to galaxies, from the material universe to abstract thought, from science to religion. Let us not leave any stone unturned until we finally catch the glimpse of this illusive Entity. Let us follow His footsteps wherever their trace may lead us until we finally find His ancient abode.

If this Entity did exist and was the cause of the creation of the universe then its memory must exist in every particle of this universe. May be with different degrees of clarity but nothing should be devoid of His memory.

Thus the search now takes the form of the search for the most universal attribute that is shared by all existing systems. All things have common or universal attributes because they came out from the same source. Universality will serve now as the tool by which we may identify the source of all existing things.

What is the common property or attribute among all existing things? Is it energy in its various forms: mass, kinetic, potential, thermal, electromagnetic, nuclear...etc.? If the creation of the universe means the creation of energy, then this is a violation of the law of the conservation of energy. From where did the first jolt of energy come?

Let us introduce another quantity which I called the inverse energy (or ygrene) Y:

$$Y = 1 / E$$

In the beginning and before the creation of the universe there was no energy (or matter or even space) that is to say the total energy $E = 0$. While this absolute zero value of energy may indicate that nothing did exist, the corresponding infinite value of

Y indicates that the First Entity must have created the most abundant quantity of this mysterious attribute. Moreover the creation of the universe and energy must have originated from the smallest unit or minimum limit of Y. The minimum limit of Y corresponds to the maximum limit of E. If the universe is finite and its total energy is finite, then the smallest unit of Y that was the source of the whole universe must have a non-zero value. If Y is related to the memory of this primordial entity, then this memory must persist and must not be completely erased during or after the moment of creation. The finitude of the total energy of the universe is a prerequisite for the persistence of the memory of its prior. All we need now is to become acquainted with this property Y, establish its relationship with the notion of Memory and Time.

One of the greatest attributes of energy is the multiform it may assume and the way it may be transformed from one form into another. In fact the several branches of physics are based on the establishment of these transformations: mass to energy of radiation, thermal to kinetic or electrical, nuclear to thermal and so on. Thus we may paraphrase the famous words of Heraclitus: "All things are in exchange for fire and fire for all things, as gold for merchandise and merchandise for gold" and instead we may say: "All things are in exchange for energy and energy for all things".

But after 2500 years our knowledge must have

advanced even a little from the time of Heraclitus. We must not repeat the same ideas even if we use different and modern terminology. If we could have interrogated Heraclitus we should have asked him: but from where did this primordial fire come? What was its source? Why do you attribute to this fire permanence and eternity? Does the source of change is unchangeable? The only constant is change. Isn't that a contradiction?

There must be a prior to fire and energy. This prior must possess a property which is the opposite or the inverse of energy, so that if energy is the cause of change in our universe then this property guarantees the permanence of its source. Thus at the moment of the creation of the universe one unit or a quantum of the Primordial Entity was annihilated and the total energy of the universe was created from its transformation. This unit or quantum is the absolute One. It is a one in the sense that the whole universe came out of it. But it is also a one because it is the unit of the primordial universe or the archetype cosmos. Since there is no division or differentiation between parts in this monad then we may not attribute any change within it.

The history of physics is related to the study of the structure of matter from atoms to elementary particles as well as the changes in these structures. Energy took an important role after the quantum revolution at the beginning of the twentieth century. The first step in this direction was taken by Max Planck when he introduced the concept of the quantization of the energy of radiation. This simple step revolutionized all of modern physics. Now we may think of energy quanta the same way we treat material particles. However no one has yet asked the questions: from where did this energy come? Or what was prior to energy? Or are there more basic and simpler entities that are the sources of the quanta of energy? We answered similar questions concerning matter when the structure of atoms, nuclei and elementary particles were discovered. However the question: Is there any prior (logical and temporal) to the quanta of energy has never been asked.

In his work on Metaphysics, Aristotle was searching for the substance of all things that exist. Can we confidently solve his problem by saying that energy is the substance of all existing things? or equivalently can anything exist without possessing some form of energy such as mass, kinetic, electromagnetic, gravitational or nuclear energy? The substance of all things must be permanent and simple. Perhaps we have to change the meaning of the words creation and annihilation, as Leibniz stated, since the annihilation of a particle and antiparticle does not mean the annihilation of any energy but the transformation of their mass into energy of radiation. Systems may transform their appearances but their total energy must be conserved. However if we consider now the moment of the creation of the whole universe we have to face the question: From where did its total energy come? Out of nothing? Is the law of conservation of energy which held firm in all processes of nature to be violated only at this single moment, the moment of the creation of the universe? Is the substance of the universe (energy) not conserved since it did not exist before the moment of creation? If there is an eternal substance underlying the substance (energy) of the universe, then this substance must have existed even before the creation of the universe. The energy of the universe is just a transformation of this substance such as mass and energy are the transformations of each other according to Einstein's relation. We need to know the nature and attributes of this primordial entity or substance.

The first step is to prove the necessity of the existence of an unchanging and therefore eternal substance. We may remark that since energy is the source of every change, it cannot be this unchanging and eternal substance. A thing must be consistent with itself or its own nature; as an example fire produces heat. Therefore a changeless substance cannot be the source of movement and change.

Let us define a quantity Y as the inverse of the energy E. If energy is the source of change then the inverse of energy Y must be the source of changelessness or permanence. However we do not observe any object which is absolutely permanent. But this does not imply that the property Y does not exist because:

1. It may have existed in the past, even the remotest past before the creation of the universe.

2. Things may have only relative permanence that is to say may possess only a finite value of the property Y which may happen to be exceedingly small.

3. This entity must be related to past time and memory, since the past cannot be changed.

But Y is not material. It is the substance of energy itself as the energy may be considered as a substratum of mass. The property Y is a measure of the lack or absence of E. Therefore before the creation of the universe ($E = 0$) this property must have assumed an infinite value. But since this substance must always be in the past of every subsequent state of the universe since its creation then it must be intimately related to past time. Therefore this First Entity must be the Universal Time which produced our ordinary time and with it the universe itself.

What are the attributes of this pre-existing substance or Entity? The Entity which produced the material universe at the moment of creation cannot itself be material.

Why this Primordial Entity produced the universe at this particular moment but not before or after? Why this Entity produced the universe at all and did not remain in an eternal repose without any change including this act of the creation of the universe?

These questions imply that an Entity had existed presumably from eternity and in the "fullness" of time a part of this entity was transformed into energy which produced the whole of the present universe. But was it necessary to produce the universe? Could it have remained throughout all eternity without such transformation? Did it produce other universes perhaps infinite in number? Could it have produced a different universe or ours is a unique and its structure is inevitable?

Let us start from the beginning.

To exist is the same as to be. But one may ask: To be what? The answer is to be itself or to maintain its identity. To maintain its identity means to have certain degree of permanence or persistence. Therefore Existence must be the degree of permanence or stability. To maintain its identity requires memory. But memory implies Time.

Also permanence and stability are the opposite of change. Therefore the degree of existence is the same as the degree of the lack of change or the degree of changelessness.

The inverse energy Y is the measure or the degree of existence. The First Being must have the highest degree of existence. It is infinite in its being.

Is Y a continuous quantity or discrete? If discrete or quantized what is its smallest unit or quantum? One may answer this question and say that Y must be quantized. The source of energy E which is quantized must have similar features or properties. In other words the energy E retains some memory of its prior and source namely quantization.

What is the unit or quantum of existence? To explain let us consider the example of Life. Although living things are made of a multitude of inanimate objects such as atoms and molecules, yet we can distinguish clearly the unit of living matter as a single cell. Now what is this unit cell of existence? If Y is inversely proportional to the energy E, therefore the minimum value of Y which we might call ΔY must correspond to the maximum value of E. But the maximum value of E implies the inclusion of the total energy of the whole universe. Therefore the quantum of existence must be encountered at the moment of the creation of the whole universe at which one quantum of the Primordial Being ΔY was annihilated and the whole universe was created out of this quantum.

Whence did this one quantum of existence come?

Let us refer once more to the example of the annihilation of a particle and an anti-particle. The breakdown of the old law of conservation of mass in this example was not a serious problem since it was replaced by a more general law, namely the law of conservation of energy. Now we ask: From where did the total energy of the universe come? We may answer this question and say it came from one quantum of the primordial substance Y. This implies that the total energy of the universe E_{total} must be finite since ΔY cannot be reduced to zero.

Now the mass in the universe came from the high energy radiation at the first few moments after the creation of the universe. Similarly this high energy came from another entity which I called the primordial substance Y. However, this series may not be extended *ad infinitum* if this primordial substance Y is permanent and through the transformation of one of its infinite number of quanta into energy the universe was created. While the whole universe came out of one quantum of Y, the totality of Y, which has an infinite number of such quanta, corresponds to $E = 0$. Therefore the totality of Y cannot be material, though its smallest parts or units are the source of all energy and matter in the universe. This situation does not represent the void or nothingness but absolute permanence and eternity. The very existence of the universe came from the lower limit of the primordial substance Y, while the unlimited totality of Y must represent the vanishing of the material universe and the establishment of the permanent and eternal universe which I called the archetype cosmos.

But did the Primordial Substance create only energy or did it create Time as well?

The Primordial Substance is the storehouse of an Archetypal Time. It has been said that you may see the whole universe in a grain of sand. Similarly you may unfold the whole history of a universe from one quantum of the Primordial Substance. Leibniz said that each monad contains representation of the whole universe.

But we do not see in our universe time transforming into energy. This is because this process of transformation requires at least one quantum of the primordial substance which transforms into a whole universe. This Archetypal Time is not our familiar time. It is a quantized co-existing form of time that predated our universe with its continuous and sequential time.

Time is an exchange for energy and energy for time as mass for energy and energy for mass. The First Being is the Eternal that created infinite quanta of the Primordial Time. Each corresponds to a possible universe. The First Being is infinitely creative. We know now why nothing else could have been created. All possible creations have already been made in the Archetype Cosmos. We just live in one of these possibilities. We also know why each being is granted only a finite duration. God is the only Infinite One and every other entity must be finite and consequently must be material and changeable.

CHAPTER 4
CREATION OF THE UNIVERSE

We may capture the faint glimpse of God when we study the most advanced concepts in Mathematics, Physics and Biology. In Mathematics the concept of infinity is the highest concept which we will encounter in the search for the Primordial Substance with its infinite number of quanta of time. Also we will use the concept of the One when we treat the whole universe as originating from one single quantum of this primeval field. We learn from Physics the idea of the transformation of a photon or a quantum of electromagnetic field into massive particles. This is the closest analogy one may think of when considering the creation of the universe out of one quantum of the incorporeal primeval field. However in order to comprehend how the infinite number of quanta of the Primordial Substance assumes properties different from and even opposite to those of the material universe and does not even contain any energy or matter, there is no better example to explain this than the brain-mind analogy. Although the mind is not a material entity yet it is rooted in this biological organization of billions of neurons which we call the brain. So let us start from the beginning and see how these concepts in mathematics, physics and biology may help us to comprehend the incomprehensible Primary and First Being whom we call God.

George Lemaitre introduced the idea of a primeval atom which contained all matter in the universe before the moment of creation. This primeval atom exploded and was pulverized at the moment of creation in what we call now the big bang. The recent progress in the study of the early universe changed our understanding of the nature of the constituents of the early universe during its first few moments. At this epoch we cannot speak of matter or atoms. The extremely high temperature did not allow matter to exist in its present state. The earliest state which we may speak of is energy in the form of radiation. However the idea of a unit or a quantum of some sort which predated our cosmos may still be maintained and may replace the idea of the primeval atom which was the origin of all energy and matter in the universe today as explained below.

From where did this primeval quantum come? Could it be that the jolt of energy which was the origin of all the galaxies and the dust in the universe is but one quantum of a field which predated our universe? In other words could our universe be just the transformation of one quantum of this primeval field? We have to get acquainted with the properties of this parent field and specially the process by which one of its infinite quanta was transformed into our universe. An example from physics may illustrate this situation: a quantum of electromagnetic field or a photon could be transformed into an electron and a positron in the process of the creation of this particle-antiparticle pair. In this example the energy of this quantum of radiation or photon is transformed into the masses of these two particles according to Einstein's energy-mass formula. The nature of the original electromagnetic field is quite different from the nature of the massive particles produced in this process. In a similar way we would like to learn about the nature of the parent field which created our universe through the transformation or annihilation of one of its quanta into the high energy radiation at the moment of creation.

The nature of any field is determined by the collective properties of its quanta which is infinite in number. The transformation of one of the quanta of this field into our universe means that the number of quanta in the original field is not conserved. However if the number of such quanta is infinite, then the loss of one or more of its quanta does not change the parent field in any way. Thus we may have a process of creation which does not change or diminish the original entity that created the universe. The infinite number of quanta of the primeval field solves the problem of the conservation of energy I discussed earlier. The primeval field remains unchanged with a total of zero energy (as will be explained below) even after imparting the whole energy of the universe through the transformation of one of its quanta.

If the whole universe came from one quantum of this primeval field at the moment of its creation, then this quantum must contain the total amount of energy to be found in the universe assuming that our universe is finite in mass and energy. However the word quantum is usually used to refer to the smallest quantity of a certain entity. How then can we use the same word "quantum" to refer to the smallest amount of this entity and at the same time to the largest or total quantity of energy to be found in the whole universe? Here the quantum we are discussing must refer to a quantum or unit of another entity different from energy. As a matter of fact this entity must be the inverse of energy such that the maximum amount of energy to be found in the universe must correspond to the minimum amount of this entity of the primeval field. Thus the first feature of the parent field we are seeking is starting to be manifested through a quantity or a property which is the inverse of energy. Each of the units or quanta of this field must possess the total energy of a possible universe. The infinite number of quanta in this field corresponds to an infinite number of possible universes.

Now if the property we are seeking in this parent field is the inverse of the energy found in our universe, then this original field or universe seems to be an Inverse Universe. The totality of the infinite number of quanta constituting this field must correspond to absolute zero energy. This means that this field or archetype cosmos has no energy or matter because:

$$\Delta Y = 1 \, / \, E_{univ}$$

Thus the sum of the total number of quanta in this field is given by:

$$Y = \Sigma \, \Delta Y = 1 \, / \, E$$

where E_{univ} is the total finite energy of a possible universe and the summation in the last equation is over an infinite number of quanta ΔY. Therefore Y must be infinite and consequently $E = 0$ as stated above.

What kind of a universe is this archetype cosmos which does not contain any energy or matter? This archetype cosmos must be an immaterial universe made up of an entity which is both logically and temporally prior to energy and matter. We have here two candidates for such entity, namely space or time (or both). However, a quantum by definition must be proportional to (the reduced) Planck's constant $\hbar$ and inversely proportional to energy as stated above. Therefore, by dimensional analysis these quanta must have the dimensions of time and we may rewrite the above equation for ΔY for one of such quanta in the form of Planck's relation as follows:

$$\tau = \hbar / E_{univ}$$

Here the archetype cosmos consists of infinite time-like quanta. The sum of an infinite number of these quanta must represent an entity which includes all possible time lines or histories: past, present and future for all possible universes in a standing repose. Change is due to the transition from one moment of time to the next in our familiar sequential time. But when we consider all of time simultaneously stored in these quanta, then no change can ever take place. We must not visualize these quanta of time as if being distributed throughout space. Time and space are mutually exclusive. Time does not exist in space. In this case time is prior to space. The quanta of time must have their own abstract space. The closest example to illustrate this abstract space is our own memories which contain only past times. However this Universal Memory which is the archetype cosmos must contain all time: past, present and future for all possible universes. The absence of space in the primeval field may explain why the size of the universe was infinitesimal at the moment of its creation. It emerged from a realm in which there was no space. Later space would emerge as extremely small entity and then grows larger with the passage of Time as the universe expands. Space acquires its magnitude with the passage of time.

In this archetype cosmos made up of an infinite number of time-like quanta each represented by τ there is no passing away of time. The whole of time co-exist simultaneously. Each quantum contains the whole history of a possible universe consequently the potential of the unfolding of its history. Thus the Primordial Substance may be described by paraphrasing the words of the prophet Daniel: "The Ancient of Days", and according to our present theory we may even describe Him as: "The Infinite of Days", considering τ to represent the units of Time or days according to our common language. So far we found that the primordial substance must have absolute zero energy and consists of an infinite number of time-like quanta and consequently in this Universal Memory there is no passing away of time or fading away of memory. The Primeval Substance must be an Eternal Being.

The relationship between each of these quanta (such as the one which produced our own universe) and the

Eternal Being is very crucial in order to understand our relationship with this Higher Being. This relationship may be illustrated using the analogy of an individual cell in our body and the whole body. Each cell contains DNA molecules which hold the code of information of the whole body in the form of a specific sequence of its nucleotides or bases. Thus some of its genes may determine the color of the eyes or the size of the brain ...etc. Similarly each quantum of the primeval field contains the code of the Eternal Being as a whole through the unfolding of the sequence of events in its local time which represents its own history. Some of these events are the creation of the universe, the beginning of life on earth and the appearance of man possessing intelligence and consciousness. Here I used the spatial sequence of the bases of the DNA molecule as an analogy for the temporal sequence of events in the history of the universe. Thus through our own experience in time we may discover the nature and the attributes of the Eternal Being. All of our experiences through the unfolding of the history of the universe contain the "code" of the First Being. We may decipher the nature of the First Being if we analyze and comprehend our own life and experience.

Our understanding of everyday phenomena around us is due to the narrow window by which we experience the passage of time, one moment at a time. We are confined within one quantum of this mysterious parent field which consists of an infinite number of quanta. If we can break the chains which confine our thinking and imagination and ascend to the realm of the totality of existence, to the realm of the infinite number of quanta of Time, we would have a completely different perspective of reality. In such a universe there is no matter or energy or even space and time in its ordinary sense. What we call time is nothing but the unfolding and thus the partial experience of one quantum of the whole of Time. If we arrive at the storehouse of the Primordial Time we would have no experience of the passage of time. As if we experience the passage of time due to our incomplete possession of this same entity or due to the partial experience of it. Then in order to come to grasp with the true nature of the Eternal Being we have to become aware of the limitations of our own experience due to our imperfect knowledge.

To illustrate the difference between the one unit or quantum of time and the totality of the Primordial Time we may refer back to the difference between one neuron and the complete network of such neurons constituting our brains. In the study of neurons there is no place for such ideas as free will, love, compassion and so on. These neurons follow the strict laws of electrochemical processes, i.e. according to the laws of physics and chemistry. However the complete network made up of some hundred billion of such neurons constituting the brain is something totally different. Here we encounter the non-material ideas of the Mind such as ethics, justice, beauty...etc. This example serves just as an illustration of the difference between Matter and Mind. Similarly, the consideration of the totality of the First Being with its infinite number of time quanta, each representing a potential universe, is a concept beyond matter, energy or space. If we want to use our familiar notions in order to describe this entity approximately we may consider it as being composed of quanta of Time. However this Time is not our everyday experienced time but rather an abstract Time. Thus the Eternal Being stands in a relationship to our universe in an approximate resemblance to the relationship between the Mind and a single neuron. The Eternal Being is thus the Divine Mind which transcends the whole universe. This view is sharply different from pantheism which equates God with the universe. Unless we can equate the brain to the Mind and even far worse if we can equate one neuron to the Mind.

Those infinite number of time-like quanta in their own abstract space representing infinite number of possible universes and in them is found all Time, past, present and future. When we behold them in our thought we behold God "who is, and was and is to come". In our own time and throughout the unfolding of the history of our own universe, the nature of this

Authentic Time is hidden. If we can understand the meaning of the events scattered along our own history, we may come a little closer to comprehend the reality of this higher Time. As T. S. Eliot said, "Only through time, time is conquered".

Thus we may consider time as the umbilical cords between all existents and the First Being. For this reason each individual being must look back in time to the Initial State of the Universe, where he may achieve a contact with the Eternal Being. But looking back in time means that every being must possess some memory of the First Being. The Initial State of the universe must always be in the past of every subsequent state. For an entity to exist it must stretch towards the past in an attempt to reach to this ultimate reality. However, due to the finite memory of all beings they fall short of making a complete contact with the First Being.

Now how was the universe created?

The First Being abode is in an archetype cosmos consisting of an infinite number of simple substances or monads. These units of being are time-like quanta which co-exist simultaneously rather than unfold sequentially like our familiar time. The first act of the First Being is to generate these Time quanta. Consequently this act of generation must have been prior and beyond time. It is an eternal act. Time is the outcome of this act. Each one of these quanta contains a representation in the form of a memory of the First Being. One of these infinite primordial quanta was chosen to generate our own universe. This act of selecting one out of an infinite number of possible alternatives is to be repeated again in choosing one structure of molecules out of an infinite number of possible structures to produce life. Then one form of life is chosen to possess intelligence that is the human being. Since this monad was created, it must also be liable to be annihilated as Leibnitz said. Thus it came to the end of its existence. It must be a finite entity unlike its source, the First Being which is the only infinite Being. It died out and its substance (time) was transformed to become the substance of the universe in the form of the high energy radiation of the early universe.

However the lingering memory of the Primordial Cosmos with its infinite number of quanta can still be seen in the multitude of photons or quanta of energy of radiation at the first few moments after the creation of the universe. Although these quanta of energy mimic the time-quanta generated by the First Being, yet they differ from them in quality and quantity since they are material in nature and finite in number.

CHAPTER 5
LIFE

How did Life start on earth? Why certain molecular structures are necessary and universal among all forms of living organisms? Is the information stored in the basic molecular structures of living organisms innate in these structures and was originally generated by these molecules or was it transmitted to them from an immaterial external source? In other words is the material structure prior to the information of life or vice versa? What is the purpose of Life?

It is well known that the DNA (deoxyribonucleic acid) structure is the fundamental macromolecule that is shared by almost all living organisms. It is one of two types of polymers known as nucleic acids (the other one is the RNA or ribonucleic acid). The structure of the DNA consists of a backbone strands made of alternating molecules of phosphates and sugars in the form of a double helix. There are also bases that cross from one strand of the double helix to the other. The bases in the DNA are adenine (A), thymine (T), guanine (G) and cytosine (C). In the RNA the thymine (T) is replaced by Urecil (U). These bases are paired together such that G must pair with C and A must pair with T. Each of these bases is anchored to one strand of the double helix by bonding with the sugar molecule. The monomers (units) of these polymers are called nucleotides.

Some of the structural characteristics of this double helix are the following:

1. Each strand of the double helix (the backbone part, without the bases) is a right hand helix (except in Z-DNA conformation) with alternating sugar and phosphate molecules. This regular repetition along a strand of the double helix represents a periodic structure of considerable length (millions or perhaps billions of units).

2. The two strands run in opposite direction to each other (anti-parallel). Each strand has a specific direction (called 5'-3'). Thus suppose one strand starts from 5' and ends at 3' then the other strand has its 5' end at the 3' of the first strand and its 5' end at the 3' of the first strand.

3. At their ends the two strands of the double helix join

together by a loop of molecules known as telomeres. Thus the whole structure represents a closed loop of specific direction made of alternating molecules of phosphate and sugar strands with the bases crossing from one strand to the other.

4. Any break in the backbone strands or the detachment of the end telomeres molecules will disrupt the function of the whole DNA macromolecule.

The periodic structures of crystalline solids are studied extensively in solid state physics. One of the well known theories in this field shows that electrons may propagate through these periodic structures without any resistance. They *tunnel* through all atoms which represent the units of these structures. Another feature of periodic lattices (as they are usually called) is that electrons may only occupy specific levels of energy grouped in bands and these bands are separated from one another by energy gaps (called forbidden energy gaps since electrons cannot assume such energy levels), hence the name of the energy band theory of crystalline solids.

The study of the DNA structure and its functions is usually viewed from a static and structural point of view. No dynamical aspects of this structure has yet been investigated, although in its very fundamental function, namely in its replication and transcription of RNA some processes must be accounted for dynamically. The periodic structure of the backbone strands of the DNA suggests that a flow of electron current in the loop made up of these strands must be considered. This current flow is supported by the following observations:

1. This current may carry the information necessary for the transcription RNA.

2. It is necessary for a current flow to have a closed circuit of a conducting medium. The presence of the end telomeres molecules supports the idea of current flow in this closed loop. The unidirectional flow of this current necessitates the reverse orientation of the two helical strands (anti-parallel) such that as the current travels around this loop it flows always in the same direction in each of the two strands (say 5′ – 3′). Also any break in the backbone strands or the separation of the telomeres end molecules will disrupt the function of the whole DNA which may be considered as the result of the disruption of the flow of this current.

3. The flow of electric current in two parallel wires in opposite directions produces an attractive electromagnetic force between these two wires. Similarly a flow of an electric current around the loop consisting of the two backbone strands will produce an attractive force between the

two strands at every segment of the double helix. This will enhance its stability by making the two strands cleave to each other more tightly. On the other hand any break in these two strands or the detachment of the end telomeres molecules will switch off this current and consequently weakens the binding force between the two strands. This is a necessary step for the separation of the two strands (with bases attached to each strand) and the beginning of the replication process.

At this point it is necessary to discuss the source of the information or code carried by this electric current. An important phenomenon that will help us to understand this is known as Faraday's Induction Law in electromagnetism. Suppose we have a coil made of several turns of conducting wire. If we bring a permanent magnet close enough to this coil or insert this magnet inside the coil and then move the magnet relative to the coil (or vice versa) a voltage or an electromotive force will develop across the two ends or terminals of the coil. The polarity and amplitude of this voltage depends on the rate of change and the direction of the movement of the magnetic field relative to the coil. Now the bases of a DNA (A, T, C and G) possess permanent tiny magnets attached to their flat surfaces called magnetic moments. These magnetic moments are due to the circulation of electrons around their nuclei or molecular ring structures or due to the alignment of the spins of their electrons and nuclei. As these bases vibrate in their positions inside the double helix due to the temperature surrounding them, their magnetic fields interact with the coil-like structure of the backbone strands. This will induce a voltage which will modulate the electric current through these two strands. The strength and polarity of this current modulation depends on the strength of the magnetic moment of each base as well as its interaction with its closest neighbour bases (the two bases just above and below it). Thus the current signal produced by each base corresponds to the identity of this base as well as its two closest neighbours. This may explain why a word of three letters (such as AGT, CTG, TTA….etc) is necessary for the formation of a specific codon (the molecule that creates amino acid). This information in the current flow is carried around the loop of the whole structure of the DNA. Consequently, the whole DNA in a chromosome for example acts as a single entity rather than a collection of independent and separate genes (made up of separate stretches of strands with the bases). Since the movement of a base is the source of the current modulation at any moment of time and at the point where this base is attached to the backbone strand, then the information contained in the current depends on the sequence of these bases. The spatial sequence of bases is translated into a temporal code in this unidirectional current flow. The whole structure communicates with itself and with the outside environment through the flow of this current. The communication of information contained in the DNA with external structures, say in the transcription of RNA, is the reverse process of the generation of the current by the bases. The bases transfer their identity into a code carried by an electric current, and this current code is translated back into molecular structures in the process of the transcription of the RNA molecules. There must be a molecule that is capable of translating this electrical code into molecular structure. The RNA polymerase which generates the RNA in the transcription process must be this primeval molecule that preceded the creation of life. Unlike the DNA or RNA macromolecules there are no difficulties in mass producing such molecules naturally. These molecules may be viewed as "transducer" devices which receive electrical current signals from one of the strands of the DNA at specific points and translate the code contained in this current into a sequence of nucleotides which constitute the RNA.

From these physical and dynamical considerations the essence of Life is viewed as the flow of an electric current along the backbone strands of the DNA macromolecule carrying all the information necessary for all its functions. Thus Life is the information contained in a flow of an electric current rather than a molecular structure. The structure supports and sustains the flow of this current carrying information.

Now we may ask the question posited at the beginning of this chapter: How did Life start? Did the random aggregation of molecules generate this information of life or this information generated this structure? This is a question similar to the one posited in the last two chapters. Was there any incorporeal and immaterial cause for the creation of the material universe? Similarly we must ask here is there a necessary cause for the creation of the molecular structures of Life? This cause must as well be non-material. It must be prior to matter in all its forms. I call this cause: the Information of Life. I may mention immediately that matter cannot produce specific structures having the code of life. This is due to the fact that a "structure" of molecules means "order". However according to the second law of thermodynamics if any collection of molecules left alone by themselves without the intervention of any external source they tend to grow more and more in disordered (not ordered) states as expressed by the law of the increase of entropy. Order cannot be created spontaneously by the random movements of molecules whatever amount of time they are left alone. Thus we are left with the other alternative that the information that gave order to these molecules must have been transmitted to them by an external non-material source. Thus the first step for the creation of life requires the pre-existence of inanimate molecules that can translate this information into a structure. These molecules are the RNA polymerase molecules that must have existed before any DNA or RNA were produced. Thus no specific information or code of life had yet existed in these molecules at this stage. The first act for the creation of Life must be the imparting of information or the code of RNA formation into these polymerase molecules in the form of the flow of an electric current. This current might have been produced by lightning since a considerable amount of energy is required to raise electrons from the valence energy band (electrons are bound to individual atoms) to the conduction energy band (electrons are free to flow in the periodic structure as an electrical current) across the forbidden energy gap. The forbidden energy gap in such molecules is wide and requires a considerable amount of energy to raise electrons across it.

Once an electric current carrying the code of Life starts to flow in these RNA polymerases, they will start producing RNA's with nucleotide sequences depending on the code imparted by the current signals. These RNA's may join together to produce DNA in a process known as reverse transcription.

The flow of current carrying information through the original RNA polymerases speeds up the process of constructing the RNA macromolecules. The random rearrangements of nucleotides in order to produce a single DNA would take time longer than the age of the universe. The spark (or lightning) which imparted the code for the sequence of nucleotides in the first RNA's is thus the origin of Life on earth. This spark imparted Life to the dead molecular structures of the RNA polymerases. Therefore this information is the source and origin of Life. Life is not the structure of the macromolecule called DNA or RNA but rather the information stored in these molecules.

The information of Life imparted to the RNA polymerases by a strike of lightning became a physical structure: The Word became flesh. Once a DNA double helix was completed and its two ends were capped by two termination telomeres molecules, a current started to flow around the closed loop or circuit made up of its two strands. This current may be viewed now as an echo of the First Spark which started Life. Each DNA macromolecule in the nucleus of every living cell still echoes the first act of the creation of Life, the strike of lightning which imparted the information of Life to dead matter. When RNA polymerases molecules are attached to a DNA in order to form RNA by tapping the information contained in the electric current flowing through one of the two strands of this DNA, a re-enactment of the first act of the creation of Life is displayed. The parent DNA now takes the role of the First Spark which imparted the code of life to RNA.

If indeed it was a spark that carried the information which created the First RNA and later the DNA of the first living cell, then there could have been several of such acts to create different kinds of DNA and consequently different forms of life. The present scenario for the creation of life is much simpler and faster than random and chaotic mutations among nucleotides to construct a DNA. The species do not have to evolve one from another. This takes too long time and its final products are uncertain. The species could have been mass produced about the same time given the proper conditions. Their differences are due to specific different information imparted to the original RNA polymerase molecules not due to chance.

But the idea of information contained in an electric current or a spark of lightning may not be familiar to some people (though not to electrical engineers). How to relate electrical signals to information and Knowledge? The best answer to this question may be found in the brain. Here in this final frontier we find the same traits of the creation of Life to be repeated in the creation of the Mind. The neurons in the brain *fire* electrical pulses (called action potentials) that propagate along the axons to other neurons. These neurons (postsynaptic) in turn collect several pulses from other different neurons (pre-synaptic) and calculate when and how fast to fire other action potentials in turn and so on. These electrical activities in our brains are the essence of thought and Knowledge. Here finally we come to the ultimate goal of creation. The First Spark produced Life, Life produced the brain and the many sparks in our brains produce thought.

But how was the First Spark produced? If we consider nature and the universe as a representation and a manifestation of the Mind of God, then Life is an implementation of the Thought of God. God thought Life and immediately a Spark or lightning struck these RNA polymerase molecules imparting to them the information of Life. This is the meaning of Life. We may argue about the origin of dead matter and molecules, but thought and information must proceed from an Intelligent Being. Thought is prior to matter as being is prior to not-being. Matter cannot produce information in the form of the sequence of DNA bases. This information must be imparted to matter in the first act of the creation of Life. The multiplication of life forms from other life forms is based on the propagation and maintenance of the information imparted to matter in the first act of the creation of life. Thus this is the purpose of Life: to keep and to preserve and to propagate the First Spark which started Life on Earth. All life forms are but memory devices that store the Utterance of God.

If this is indeed the story of Life then there is nothing to fear from death. The *original copy of Life* is kept safe there in the Mind of God. Even when this molecular structure dies or is destroyed, the authentic Life, the original information, is still There. Again Life is not the *structure* but the *information* stored temporarily in this structure but eternally in the Mind of God.

Then, this is Eternal Life, the perpetual Memory or persistence of this Knowledge and information in the Mind of God which we only came to know it in its material copy or material translation and consequently in its ephemeral form. If we ascend from the material form to the Knowledge of God we will behold Life undiminished and without death. Also the Spark which started Life in the first place can rekindle this Life and resurrect it from the dead.

CHAPTER 6
KNOWLEDGE

What is *True Knowledge*?

True Knowledge is the knowledge of the *Real Being*. Not this being or that being, not in this state or another state but *Knowledge of Being* in its summit, in its repose. This Knowledge renders all other kinds of knowledge mere trivial special cases that fade away once we possess the *Source and Fountain of Knowledge*. To come across this Knowledge cannot be by chance or by trial and error or by extrapolation from our imperfect and empirical knowledge since the complete cannot be the outcome of the incomplete.

What are the attributes of *"Being"* that we seek to know? What method should we employ to possess such *Knowledge*? Is it the scientific approach, the religious experience, the artistic impression, or perhaps something else yet to be discovered? We must recall that science itself was invented as an attempt to comprehend the universe around us. Therefore we must not exaggerate the role of science as Kant did by trying to make metaphysics to "come forth as a science". We must use the tool that is adequate and fit to perform the job at hand. In reaching towards this *Ultimate Knowledge* we must stop for a moment to inquire whether science is the proper tool for this job. Could it be that science is the first step to miss our goal? Are the premises of science commensurate with this *True Knowledge*?

What we call science is in fact nothing but observations of very limited scope of a limited number of phenomena. We started to be familiar with these phenomena only very recently, a few centuries ago. Could such limited and recent source of data be applied to know the *Limitless and Eternal*? Could the experience of the very few be the reliable source to know the *Universal*? This *Ultimate Knowledge* must be manifested to everyone. Its presence must be everywhere. Its appearance must be from the dawn of history. Its representations must be apparent in science, religion, arts and in every other higher endeavors of human thought.

What are the traits that appeared at the dawn of civilization and persisted since in every major effort to comprehend reality?

The ancient Greeks were the first people to address

the problems of "Being" and the theory of Knowledge. However those Greeks had great admiration for the ancient Egyptians. Aristotle attributed the discovery of Mathematics to the priests of ancient Egypt. The civilization in the Nile valley was an inspiration for those great Greek thinkers. But what vision did those ancient Egyptians had? To what ultimate goal did they channel their tremendous energies in building their magnificent monuments?

Those monuments were not erected to verify a theory, or to test a hypothesis. Man, from the dawn of history, was responding to a mysterious force that directed his efforts to the source of *True Knowledge*. He thought first that the object of this Knowledge was to find God and to worship Him. The natural reason for that was the recognition that this God is the creator of the whole universe and all that is in it. Today with our modern cosmological theories for the creation of the universe we do not know what to do with such knowledge. There is no purpose for our knowledge. It is an impotent knowledge. There is no Master Plan behind such ideas. We do not go erecting temples and pyramids for the big bang. Perhaps we do not believe so deeply in our theories as much as the ancients did believe in their religion. The "god" of the big bang is an impersonal god, a god of chance not purpose, an empty space god not a god of Truth and Reality. The ultimate triumph of science in combining the physics of elementary particles and cosmology ended up in a blind alley. There is no hope in the big bang for eternal life, for the survival of human soul after death, even for the existence of human soul.

Notice the transformation of the revelation of *"Being"* from the time of the ancient Egyptians to the Greeks to modern time. The ancient Egyptians worshiped the Being that appeared on the primeval waters of creation, the Greeks speculated on the Idea of Being and modern scientists ignored this idea completely or at least identified it with elementary particles and the quanta of energy. From recognizing this Being as spiritual, it became intellectual idea and finally it is recognized only in the form of matter. Is this a kind of incarnation, the transformation of the Spirit into the Word and ultimately became Matter? Or perhaps it is a descent of the Supreme to the dark recesses of Matter? Is this observation speaks of the *death* of the First Being? How can we recover the original vision? How are we going to make the ascent back to the realm of the Real Being which Plato alluded to in his parable of the cave? How will the *First Being* resurrected?

To correct this negligence for human aspiration we have to revive the primordial hope of every human being to know the *First Being.* We have to ask ourselves whether science can satisfy this fundamental desire for *True Knowledge.* In our approach to solve this problem we have to violate the very first principles of science.

We have to start with what we hope for then try to find out the way to achieve it rather than to start from neutral and purposeless hypotheses and arrive at useless and meaningless conclusions. Kant started with the principles of pure reason and ended up by denying any possibility of the *Knowledge of the Ultimate Being.* He tried to apply the methods and concepts of theoretical physics and pure mathematics to this higher form of knowledge. He replaced true knowledge with a counterfeit one.

Aristotle started his treatise which came to be known as the Metaphysics by the following words: "All men by nature desire to know". In this present book I am investigating the question: What is the object of this desire to know? When God created this desire to know He must have provided the objects that satisfy this desire. This is exactly the same situation with all other desires. For example there are specific objects by which we quench our thirst or satisfy our hunger, namely water and food. Similarly I am seeking to know the elements of this particular type of knowledge that can satisfy this desire to know. Can any form of knowledge satisfy this desire, or there may be specific types of knowledge that satisfy this desire. Is there an ultimate form of knowledge according to which all science, philosophy and religion are but special branches and thus subordinate to this *Authentic Knowledge*?

How can we be sure that this form of knowledge,

assuming that it does exist, is complete, does not require change, and does not need to be updated or replaced similar to all other sciences? How to express this form of Knowledge: in mathematical equations, by the language and by the concepts of modern physics? How about arts, music and poetry for example, are these to be included as well in this *Universal Knowledge*? In other words are all forms of knowledge reducible to mathematics or physics?

No doubt there is a desire in every human being to know. We may not discern this desire clearly in many instances or confuse the object of our knowledge with substitute or pseudo-knowledge. This maneuver may quench our thirst to know for a while but sooner or later we discover that the newly acquired knowledge falls short of satisfying our needs and we embark anew on another search to obtain more or different kind of knowledge. This process may go on and on throughout the lifetime of an individual or even from generation to generation. The ancient Greek thinkers were the first to discern this dilemma and thought to find out the *True Knowledge* or the *Changeless Truth* that is behind the ever changing phenomena. Some other thinkers (the skeptics) reached the opposite conclusion that either such sort of knowledge does not exist or it is impossible to obtain.

We must consider a form of knowledge beyond what we used to call knowledge in everyday language.

We use this word to replace an original word. Our ordinary usage of this word means the knowledge of the transient and finite. Our everyday knowledge is a partial knowledge. This other *True Knowledge* is complete and unchangeable. Once we acquire it we do not forget it or replace it.

The completeness of this knowledge puts severe restrictions that cannot be satisfied by any other kind of knowledge. Also the object of this knowledge must be out of this world since any object in this world is finite and ephemeral. Only stable and unchanging objects can lend themselves to perfect and true knowledge.

But if this knowledge is about things out of this world does this make it useless knowledge. Many people would discard it. They hold that this world is all that is. Either there is nothing outside it or we are unable to know and verify any other kind of knowledge that deals with things beyond this world. In short most of modern scientist do not subscribe to metaphysics. However if we show that metaphysics is inseparable from physics and is necessary as its foundations then there is no escape from accepting its claims even if this task seems to be a very difficult one.

In modern times this concrete knowledge is most clearly demonstrated in pure mathematics and to some extent in modern theoretical physics. But at the same time many thinkers discovered that the different branches of knowledge started to diverge and it became more and more difficult to combine all these branches of knowledge under one encompassing Science or Philosophy or under any other name. A schism developed in human thought and knowledge as it is apparent between the two fields of physics and metaphysics. The object of these two branches of knowledge may be defined approximately by:

1. Matter is the subject of physics.
2. Mind or Thought or God is addressed by the Theory of Knowledge and by Metaphysics.

Is there one unified theory or Principle that combine these two branches of knowledge or the schism expressed by Descartes between Mind and Body must always remain and surface in any critical analysis and investigation of knowledge?

This question may be put in a different form as follows: What is the Idea or Principle that is logically prior to Knowledge and is the common denominator among all beings?

Any *a priori* principle must be necessary and universal among all beings. Therefore in order to reconcile the schism of human thought we must ascend to the First and the Primary and the Universal Principle by which all things have their existence and at the same time are amenable to be known and comprehended. So far we reached the conclusion that we must analyze both the ideas of existence and knowledge in order to find their prior.

To exist means to persist at least for a while before changing to something else or to vanish completely (if this is at all possible). In its extreme form this definition means that an entity may exist for an interval of time before ceasing to be or going out of existence. In other cases this means simply to change. For example a green leaf on a tree ceased to exist in a sense when its color changes. However it may be thought to exist in a different form (as a yellow leaf, for example). Even when this leaf falls from the tree and is decomposed we may still think of its existence as the persistence of its constituting matter. Therefore the aforementioned definition by its generality allows us to include in it a wide range of phenomena. At the same time it encompasses non-material objects as well. For example the ideas included in this book exist as long as I (the author) believe in them and do not change them. The moment I change my mind and believe in a different set of ideas then these ideas do not exist (at least as related to me). In the same sense we call some beliefs or languages to exist and are alive as long as some people believe in them or speak such languages. On the other hand some ideas, religions, or languages are considered dead when no more people practice them.

From this discussion we come to the conclusion that there are two closely related ideas to the idea of

Existence, namely: Time and Change. To exist means to exist in Time as Heidegger amply clarified. On the other hand to exist means to persist without Change. The idea of Change is the opposite to the idea of Permanence or Persistence or Existence. The True Being must be the Changeless as Parmenides said.

To go back to our problem: What is the idea or principle that is prior to the ideas of Being and Knowledge? What is the entity that encompasses both the notions of Matter and Mind? We came to the conclusion (with an agreement with Heidegger again) that this idea is Time. But what was there before time? This is an illegitimate question since before Time we may not use the proposition "before". Since Time is the most *"a priori"* notion, then it is logical not to consider any other notion to contain it or pre-exist before it. Consequently Time must have existed from an everlasting past and will continue to exist to all future eternity. Time must be an infinite quantity. However we know that the universe started at a certain moment of time. And if the universe remains forever, then this makes all the history of the universe to be a semi-infinite quantity. Thus the history of the universe is a part of total Time. The material universe exists only during the sequential phase of time. The Archetype Cosmos must exist during an earlier phase of a different type of Time: the Simultaneous co-existence of the infinite quanta of Time.

T. S. Eliot expressed the desire for the search for the source of all things whether matter or thought by the following words:

We shall not cease from exploration
And the end of all our exploring
Will be to arrive where we started
And know the place for the first time
Through the unknown, remembered gate
When the last of earth left to discover
Is that which was the beginning
At the source of the longest river

The longest river in the world is the river Nile which flows through North Africa from its sources in Lake Victoria in central Africa and Lake Tana in Ethiopia. Perhaps T.S. Eliot may have used the metaphor of a river to refer to Time and its beginning. Time has been described as a river by many thinkers. Its ceaseless flow no doubt is the motive behind this analogy. Thus we may extend this metaphor to help us in the search for the source of Time. In the metaphor of the river Nile, Lakes Victoria and Tana are the reservoirs of water that feed the flow of this river. The still waters of these great lakes are the source from which the running waters of the Nile flow. Similarly we must seek the infinite reservoir of the standing-still of All Time from which the flow of time in our universe started by the creation of the universe and still flowing ever since.

There is only one possibility that holds the promise for some success in our search. Emanuel Kant reached a similar conclusion at the end of his Prolegomena. This is the fact that the Source is connected with its offspring as the boundary to an area that is included within it. The First remains immanent in the secondary and tertiary as Plotinus reiterated many times in his Enneads. Therefore the path to the First Being is navigable. Through the river of time we can reach the source of Time. We, the explorers, bear witness to this fact. Our desire to know the First implies that we carry within us His memory which continually directs our thoughts towards Him. This is a kind of a field to which we respond by orienting our thoughts to specific ideas not unlike a compass in a magnetic field. The existence of a figure in plane geometry is determined by its boundaries. Without these bounding lines and curves a figure has no existence. The only boundary of time is the moment of creation. If there is any hope for mankind to meet with God then we must come to this sacred and holy ground, the Initial State of the Universe, where we may see God as I explained in a previous chapter. Thus the road is decided and the goal is set. What we have to do is to embark on this pilgrimage. We do not have to worry about what to take with us on this journey. On the contrary we have to drop lots of baggage, old theories and beliefs, prejudices and biases, in order to make the journey possible and enjoyable. Along the road to our Destination we will meet luminaries of past and present thinkers. Many people have gone before us on this same journey. As a matter of fact all people who ever lived embarked on this journey even if they did not know it. All human life is but a pilgrimage to meet with God. We are similar to those ancient Israelites heading towards the mount of Sinai for an appointment to meet with God. What Red sea should we cross? What kind of a promised land are we heading to?

True Knowledge is the knowledge that will replace all partial knowledge. It is the knowledge which once acquired will remain with us and can never be lost or forgotten with the passage of time. This knowledge will satisfy our desire to know. It is the true nourishment that will give new life to our minds. No more we may go searching to satisfy this desire to know. Once we obtain it our minds will become the fountain and the source that will overflow abundantly with this knowledge. It will reshape our minds in such a way that instead of being passive and only recipients of knowledge they will become active and the source of this knowledge.

If this *Knowledge* is so important, then we may pay any price, suffer any hardship and search for it in every place until we finally find it and lay hold on it and do not let it slip from our grasp. But how would we recognize it upon our first encounter? What is the sign that may indicate its presence? The Sign is this: When we hear its words we shall remember and become awoken. We shall recognize its voice and we shall know the Speaker. The words of *True Knowledge* are active and give life and intelligence to their hearers. Those words created the universe, imparted life into dead matter, created intelligence in primitive people and were the foundations of civilized societies. The sum of its words is the history of human thought. The meanings of these words are understood in all languages. Let us learn them and remember their ancient dialect. Let every thought be stilled and every idea be suspended until we recite the whole Hymn: this magnificent Hymn. Its words are sweet in our mouth. Their rhyme is not alien to our ears. We heard these words before.

Chapter 7
The First Being

I

THE ONE DAY OF CREATION is a single and Eternal Day. Its *Night* and *Daylight* are the two sides of eternity.

In the beginning it was *Night*. Everything was calm and quiet. The firmament of the archetype cosmos was studded with the primeval stars of being. These co-existent quanta of time are not in motion and are not in space. They are immovable and do not change. The Mist of Time is full and saturated with the representations of the First Being.

The moment of creation is the moment of Sunrise of this glorious and Eternal Day. One of the primeval substances was separated from the infinite *All*. It became finite and was transformed into energy. The

Primeval Sun rose from the heart of this quantum; shuttered it and scattered it; and the fragments of the primordial matter escaped to the farthest reaches of space from the face of this rising Sun:

Hail to thee Primeval Sun in thy rising
Thou created all things in that morning
Thy glorious rays, thy hands of creation, are lightning
Imparting Divine Knowledge, and dead matter
quickening

Thus the One Day of Creation consists of three consecutive epochs of time:

1. Night or the time of rest in which there was no *change or a shadow of turning.*
2. Sunrise, or the moment of creation in *which all things were created.*
3. Day, or the time of change which may be resembled by *a rushing mighty wind* that swept everything in the universe setting them in motion and in a state of flux.

This *TRION* in the One Day of Creation is the foundation upon which we must build our knowledge of the universe and the understanding of our place in it.

Our days and nights are but miniature images of this One and Eternal Day. We exist in both cycles: the little cycle and the Eternal One. That is why we are both mortal and immortal at the same time. Our lives are finite similar to our days on earth while our souls are immortal because they live in and belong to the Eternal Day of Creation.

II

Time is the manifestation of the First Being. Thus time must inherit the attributes of this Being. As we have seen the First Being is infinite. Consequently Time must also be an infinite entity. However there are two types of infinity: the countable (numerical) infinity which may be used to describe the infinite number of the simultaneously co-existing quanta of time prior to the moment of creation and the infinite extension of continuous time which represents the successive indivisible moments of time posterior to the moment of creation.

Thus we may think of all of time as composed of two distinct epochs: one prior to the moment of creation in a quantized form and another posterior to the moment of creation in a continuous and consecutive form as a one dimensional axis extending from the moment of creation to positive infinity. The point of origin (t = 0) on this axis separates the two dissimilar forms of time: the co-existent quanta of time part and the consecutive time part which has a semi-infinite extension or duration. The notion of a semi-infinite quantity (or a ray) is well known in mathematics and lends itself naturally to the description of the duration of time after the moment of creation; which I called the Day of the One Day of Creation.

Thus the universe was not created after the elapse

of an infinite period of time, which is a problem in metaphysics, since there was no ordinary sequential time before the moment of creation. Every moment of time in that prior epoch was independent of every other moment. None of them was before or after any other. All of them co-existed simultaneously.

We may ascribe to the two epochs of time prior and posterior to the moment of creation opposite states such as: Rest and Motion; Night and Day; and quantized and continuous time. The moment of creation itself was a moment of annihilation in which one quantum of the primordial field was annihilated. Thus we may consider the moment of creation as a moment of inversion in which every aspect of the archetype cosmos prior to the moment of creation became its opposite or inverse in our universe. In particular Time became its inverse or Energy as expressed by the formula given before.

THE FIRST BEING

III

At the moment of creation, one of the time-like quanta of the Changeless Archetype Cosmos became changeable. This *One* quantum became *many* photons of energy. The wholeness of this primordial *Monad* gave place to a multitudinous universe. From now on Reality will be shuttered and scattered across the whole field of Existence.

To search for the *Authentic Reality* we must therefore, gather together its scattered fragments into a one complete form of knowledge. We must not let our attention be divided now on this part of the universe, now on another part, sometimes on this phenomenon, and other times on another one, the way scientific research is carried out. This approach of acquiring partial knowledge will never lead us to know the truth about anything. The *Authentic Reality* will always be slipping away from us, or more accurately we will be drifting away from it since it never changes.

We must therefore, return back to the Source of Knowledge, to the archetype cosmos of the Monads, where we may find all things gathered together, compact without void, full of being, where there is no trace of non-being. All of the non-being is without. This form of knowledge is our Lost Paradise.
It is our Sabbath, our Day of Rest.

However, as I mentioned before, we may call it the Night of Rest that was prior to the moment of creation.

Perfect knowledge is the knowledge of the One. It cannot be increased or updated or revised. It cannot be reached by trial and error or even by observation of transient phenomena during a finite period of time. It is the true knowledge for all time including the time before the creation of the universe.

True knowledge manifests itself through its power of transforming us into the Image of the First Being. It is the way to this Being and it is the First Being Himself, the *Word*, at the same time.

The fruit of the tree of knowledge declares the nature of this tree. Is it the tree of *Life* or the tree of death?

THE FIRST BEING

IV

How can I tell about such a wonder?
The One became Many without any surrender.
The All is one and the One the whole universe engender.
Remember the One the All for us is just a reminder.

V

The moment which separated the two epochs of time in the One Day of Creation must have a special importance for all those who seek to know the fundamental truth about our universe. This moment is shrouded with ambiguity. It lies beyond the horizon of our understanding and memory. It shares the nature of its prior epoch, namely the state of absolute rest, yet it is also a part of its posterior epoch of motion and change. It is a One and Many at the same time. It combined the two opposite natures in one brief moment. It is God and Nature in One.

As if in the *fullness* of time, at the mid-point of eternity, the Primordial Quantum and the *Body* of the One was *broken* for the creation of all things in the universe. And everything that exists borrows its temporary existence from the eternal and everlasting existence of the First Being. This Primary One scattered its seeds across all the field of Time. And in its proper season it sprouted with Life. And when Life reached its maturity it produced intelligent human beings.

This mysterious event, the act of the creation of the universe, echoes throughout all of nature and history, from the spread of living organisms to the spread of civilizations. It appeared in the visions of wise men and in religious myths of ancient peoples. It is the body of Osiris torn apart and cut into pieces by his evil brother Seth and scattered all over the land of Egypt. But where to find Isis, his devoted wife, to gathered together all the fragments of his scattered sacred body? What incantations or spells should we employ in order to bring back this fragmented reality into One and Living Reality?

It is the body of Christ that was broken for us for the forgiveness of sin and to grant us Eternal Life.

We possess within us the seeds of the First Being. We are from eternity. However, we have forgotten our ancient roots and heritage. We search here and there to find objects which may or may not contain traces of reality. Our knowledge of the external and ephemeral does not satisfy our desire to know. And the Real Being dwells in us. All what we have to do is just to remember.

This vision of the fragmented One coming back together and being resurrected must be our goal and sustenance in every act we do in our life. Gathering together Knowledge as a one complete and consistent system of reason could be the first step to take on this road.

VI

The First Being manifests Himself in every aspect of the universe from matter to life to thought. When He revealed Himself in the fullness of time, He reconciled in Himself all the essential elements of the universe by taking a material body in which full Life and Wisdom dwelt. The Word came into our world to reveal to us the Knowledge of the First Being and to remind us that He is the creator of the universe and the giver of Life and Wisdom.

While the act of the Real Being is to gather together all things into One, we on the other hand divide the wholeness of the universe into independent fragments and objects of thought in order to study each separately. Also we confine the objects of our thoughts to transient phenomena of this world thus never attain to *Perfect Knowledge*. Our knowledge must be extended to encompass the whole of the universe and in particular the Archetype Cosmos, the cause and the source of our own universe. We must consider the rest of creation to be very essential to our own being and to our ability to comprehend reality.

The Changeless Primordial Universe must be the object of our knowledge. The information we gain from the study of atomic, nuclear and elementary particle phenomena always contain elements of uncertainty. Indeed, the Changeless substance is the only object of exact knowledge. Thus the Archetype Cosmos is knowable and every state of the microcosm is uncertain and unknowable.

The Archetype Universe is the *Real Being* and every state in our universe and in particular states describing smaller domains of the universe are less real and tend towards non-being. This may explain why matter could be annihilated at the nuclear and elementary particle levels and at high speeds and energies.

The Archetype Cosmos is the Abode of the Eternal First Being, while the world of elementary particles, whatever fancy names they may be given, is the place of violent motion that leads to non-being. That is why they have exceedingly short lifetimes. The spirit which inhabits the realm of these infinitesimal and fleeting particles must be the spirit of non-being.

VII

In His words and works He is the best.
But the greatest of all when He came to rest
He stretched His arms from the East to the West
And His heart (oh His heart) bled in His chest.

+ + +

O Thou who art without motion
I lift up to thee my devotion.
Hear O Lord this supplication
Thou art the King of all creation.